D1216130

Life on the Land
INUIT ART FROM CAPE DORSET

Pomegranate

PORTLAND, OREGON A BOOK OF POSTCARDS

Pomegranate Communications, Inc.
19018 NE Portal Way, Portland OR 97230
800 227 1428   www.pomegranate.com

Pomegranate Europe Ltd.
'number three', Siskin Drive, Middlemarch Business Park
Coventry CV3 4FJ, UK
+44 (0)24 7621 4461   sales@pomegranate.com

Pomegranate's mission is to invigorate, illuminate, and inspire through art.

© 2013 Dorset Fine Arts

Pomegranate publishes books of postcards on a wide range of subjects.
Please contact the publisher for more information.

ISBN 978-0-7649-6564-7
Item No. AA777

Cover designed by Gina Bostian
Printed in Korea
26 25 24 23 22 21 20 19 18 17   12 11 10 9 8 7 6 5 4 3

To facilitate detachment of the postcards from this book, fold each card along its perforation line before tearing.

In 1956, artist James Houston came with his wife, Alma, to Cape Dorset, southwest of Baffin Island in the Canadian Arctic territory of Nunavut, as the northern service officer with the Canadian government's Department of Northern Affairs. One of his duties was to foster the production of carvings and other handcrafts by the Inuit residents. By 1959, the West Baffin Eskimo Co-operative had been formed, laying the groundwork for a legendary printmaking tradition. Today, the Co-operative's Kinngait Studios are the oldest continually operating print studios in Canada, and collectors from around the world eagerly anticipate each annual release of Cape Dorset prints.

The artists of Cape Dorset are active in the studios from fall through late spring. Diverse media are available to the printmakers—etching and aquatint, woodcut, copper engraving, and stencil—but their mainstays are stonecut and lithography. When the print editions are finished and the fine summer weather arrives, many of the artists leave the community to return to the land and their traditional camps. The Inuit are determined to retain important elements of their culture—their language and stories, their connection to the Arctic and its resources—while adapting to modern ways.

This book of postcards reproduces thirty outstanding images from over fifty years of printmaking at the Kinngait Studios.

Life on the Land: **INUIT ART FROM CAPE DORSET**

Papiara Tukiki (Canadian, born 1942)
Tundra Bear, 2012
Lithograph, 57.5 × 76.7 cm (22⅝ × 30³⁄₁₆ in.)
Printer: Niveaksie Quvianaqtuliaq

800 227 1428   WWW.POMEGRANATE.COM

Pomegranate

Life on the Land: **INUIT ART FROM CAPE DORSET**

Papiara Tukiki (Canadian, born 1942)
Spring, 2006
Etching and aquatint, 49 x 73.1 cm (19⁵⁄₁₆ x 28¾ in.)
Printer: Studio PM

800 227 1428   WWW.POMEGRANATE.COM

Pomegranate

Life on the Land: **INUIT ART FROM CAPE DORSET**

Kakulu Saggiaktok (Canadian, born 1940)
Igloo, 1979
Stonecut and stencil, 55.5 x 74.5 cm (21⅞ x 29⁵⁄₁₆ in.)
Printer: Eegyvudluk Pootoogook

800 227 1428 WWW.POMEGRANATE.COM

Pomegranate

Life on the Land: **INUIT ART FROM CAPE DORSET**

Kenojuak Ashevak (Canadian, 1927–2013)
Courting Loon, 2008
Lithograph, 56 x 76.5 cm (22$\frac{1}{16}$ x 30$\frac{1}{8}$ in.)
Printer: Pitseolak Niviaqsi

800 227 1428   WWW.POMEGRANATE.COM

Pomegranate

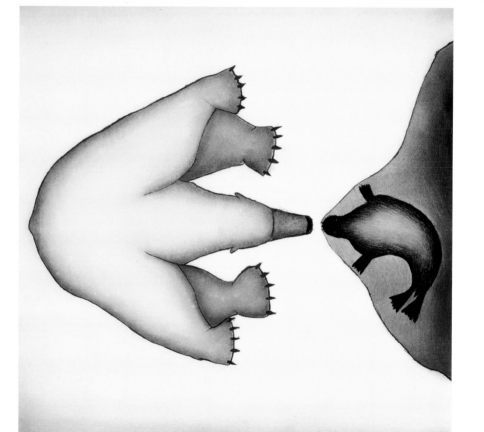

Life on the Land: INUIT ART FROM CAPE DORSET

Ohotaq Mikkigak (Canadian, 1936–2014)
Face to Face, 2009
Etching and aquatint, 62 x 57 cm (24^{7}/$_{16}$ x 22^{7}/$_{16}$ in.)
Printer: Studio PM

800 227 1428   WWW.POMEGRANATE.COM

Pomegranate

Life on the Land: **INUIT ART FROM CAPE DORSET**

Kingmeata Etidlooie (Canadian, 1915–1989)
Hunter's Dream, 1988
Lithograph, 55.5 x 76.5 cm (21⅞ x 30⅛ in.)
Printer: Pitseolak Niviaqsi

800 227 1428   WWW.POMEGRANATE.COM

Pomegranate

Life on the Land: **INUIT ART FROM CAPE DORSET**

Mary Pudlat (Canadian, 1923–2001)
Woman Gathering Kelp, 1997
Lithograph, 77 x 57 cm (30⁵⁄₁₆ x 22⁷⁄₁₆ in.)
Printer: Pitseolak Niviaqsi

800 227 1428   WWW.POMEGRANATE.COM

Pomegranate

Life on the Land: **INUIT ART FROM CAPE DORSET**

Meelia Kelly (Canadian, 1940–2006)
Colony of Seals, 2004
Stonecut and stencil, 63.7 x 76.5 cm (25$\frac{1}{16}$ x 30$\frac{1}{8}$ in.)
Printer: Qiatsuq Niviaqsi

800 227 1428   WWW.POMEGRANATE.COM

Pomegranate

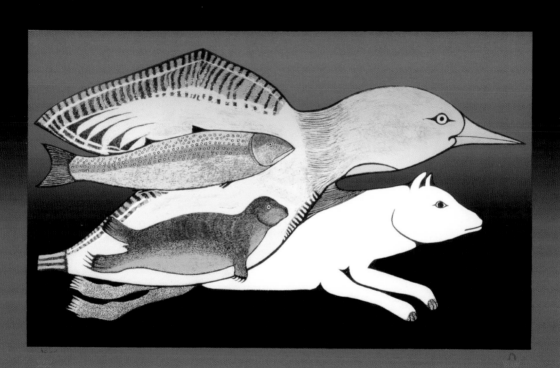

Life on the Land: **INUIT ART FROM CAPE DORSET**

Pitaloosie Saila (Canadian, born 1942)
Arctic Ensemble, 2009
Lithograph, 51 x 76.3 cm (20$\frac{1}{16}$ x 30$\frac{1}{16}$ in.)
Printer: Pitseolak Niviaqsi

800 227 1428   WWW.POMEGRANATE.COM

Pomegranate

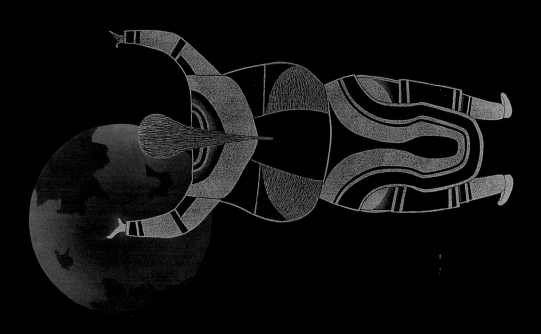

Life on the Land: **INUIT ART FROM CAPE DORSET**

Tikitu Qinnuayuak (Canadian, 1908–1992)
Woman Who Went to the Moon, 1990
Stonecut and stencil, 76 x 56 cm (29$^{15}/_{16}$ x 22$^{1}/_{16}$ in.)
Printer: Qavavau Manumie

800 227 1428   WWW.POMEGRANATE.COM

Pomegranate

Life on the Land: INUIT ART FROM CAPE DORSET

Ohotaq Mikkigak (Canadian, 1936–2014)
Aqigirq (Rock Ptarmigan), 2011
Stonecut and stencil, 58.5 x 73.5 cm (23$\frac{1}{16}$ x 28$\frac{15}{16}$ in.)
Printer: Qiatsuq Niviaqsi

800 227 1428   WWW.POMEGRANATE.COM

Pomegranate

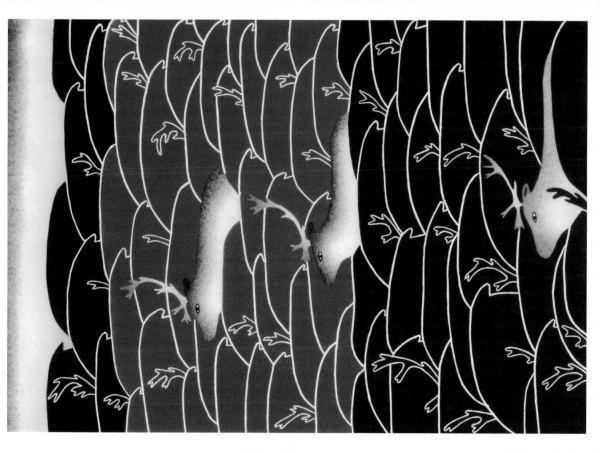

Life on the Land: **INUIT ART FROM CAPE DORSET**

Ningeokuluk Teevee (Canadian, born 1963)
Seasonal Migration, 2009
Stonecut and stencil, 76.5 x 62 cm (30⅛ x 24⁷⁄₁₆ in.)
Printer: Qiatsuq Niviaqsi

800 227 1428   WWW.POMEGRANATE.COM

Pomegranate

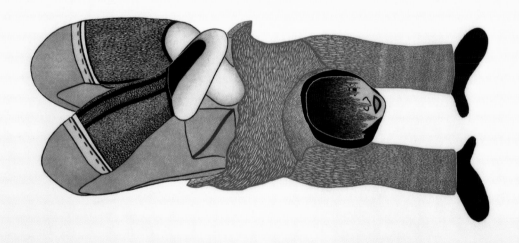

Life on the Land: **INUIT ART FROM CAPE DORSET**

Shuvinai Ashoona (Canadian, born 1961)
Handstand, 2010
Stonecut and stencil, 83.6 × 62 cm (34 × 24 $7/16$ in.)
Printer: Qiatsuq Niviaqsi

Life on the Land: INUIT ART FROM CAPE DORSET

Eegyvudluk Ragee (Canadian, 1920–1983)
Angako Quviasuktu (Happy Shaman), 1981
Stonecut and stencil, 56 x 76.5 cm (22$\frac{1}{16}$ x 30$\frac{1}{8}$ in.)
Printer: Saggiaktok Saggiaktok

800 227 1428   WWW.POMEGRANATE.COM

Pomegranate

Life on the Land: **INUIT ART FROM CAPE DORSET**

Qavavau Manumie (Canadian, born 1958)
Inugagulligaq (Legend of the Little People), 2002
Lithograph, 51.5 × 66.2 cm (20¼ × 26¹/₁₆ in.)
Printer: Pitseolak Niviaqsi

800 227 1428 WWW.POMEGRANATE.COM

Pomegranate

Life on the Land: **INUIT ART FROM CAPE DORSET**

Kenojuak Ashevak (Canadian, 1927–2013)
Vigilant Owl, 2007
Lithograph, 56.9 x 76.5 cm (22⅜ x 30⅛ in.)
Printer: Niviaksie Quvianaqtuliaq

800 227 1428 WWW.POMEGRANATE.COM

Pomegranate

Life on the Land: **INUIT ART FROM CAPE DORSET**

Kananginak Pootoogook (Canadian, 1935–2010)
Young Hunter at Aglu, 1992
Lithograph, 54.1 x 71.7 cm (21⁵⁄₁₆ x 28¼ in.)
Printer: Niviaksie Quvianaqtuliaq

800 227 1428   WWW.POMEGRANATE.COM

Pomegranate

Life on the Land: **INUIT ART FROM CAPE DORSET**

Kingmeata Etidlooie (Canadian, 1915–1989)
Northern Spirits, 1988
Lithograph, 51 x 66.5 cm (20⅟₁₆ x 26³⁄₁₆ in.)
Printer: Pitseolak Niviaqsi

WWW.POMEGRANATE.COM

800 227 1428

Pomegranate

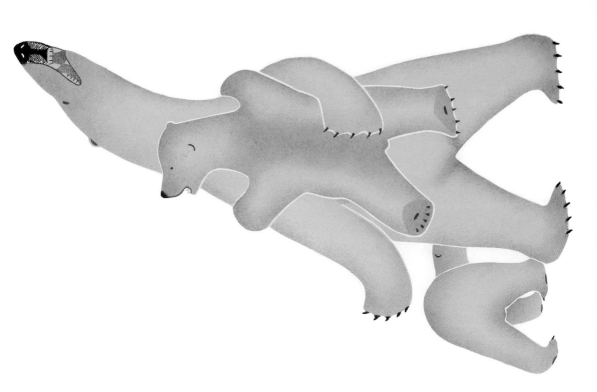

Life on the Land: **INUIT ART FROM CAPE DORSET**

Kananginak Pootoogook (Canadian, 1935–2010)
Restless Cubs, 2008
Stonecut and stencil, 62 x 49.5 cm (24$\frac{7}{16}$ x 19$\frac{1}{2}$ in.)
Printer: Qiatsuq Niviaqsi

800 227 1428   WWW.POMEGRANATE.COM

Pomegranate

Life on the Land: **INUIT ART FROM CAPE DORSET**

Qavavau Manumie (Canadian, born 1958)
Summer Treat, 2005
Stonecut and stencil, 58.5 × 66.4 cm (23$\frac{1}{16}$ × 26$\frac{1}{8}$ in.)
Printer: Qiatsuq Niviaqsi

800 227 1428   WWW.POMEGRANATE.COM

Pomegranate

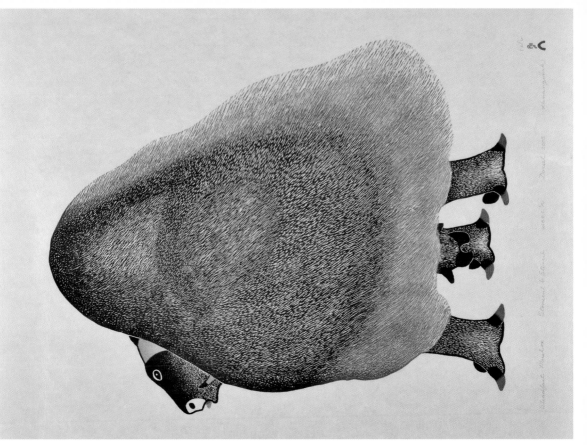

Life on the Land: **INUIT ART FROM CAPE DORSET**

Kananginak Pootoogook (Canadian, 1935–2010)
Steadfast Musk Ox, 2005
Stonecut and stencil, 62 x 49.7 cm (24$\frac{7}{16}$ x 19$\frac{9}{16}$ in.)
Printer: Qiatsuq Niviaqsi

800 227 1428 WWW.POMEGRANATE.COM

Pomegranate

Life on the Land: INUIT ART FROM CAPE DORSET

Itee Pootoogook (Canadian, 1951–2014)
Looking South, 2008
Lithograph, 30.7 x 40.8 cm (12$\frac{1}{16}$ x 16$\frac{1}{16}$ in.)
Printer: Pitseolak Niviaqsi

800 227 1428   WWW.POMEGRANATE.COM

Pomegranate

Life on the Land: **INUIT ART FROM CAPE DORSET**

Ningeokuluk Teevee (Canadian, born 1963)
Moon Dance, 2011
Stonecut and stencil, 64 x 81.2 cm ($25^3/_{16}$ x $31^{15}/_{16}$ in.)
Printer: Qiatsuq Niviaqsi

800 227 1428   WWW.POMEGRANATE.COM

Pomegranate

Life on the Land: **INUIT ART FROM CAPE DORSET**

Qavavau Manumie (Canadian, born 1958)
Spring Caribou, 1995
Etching and aquatint, 60 x 68.9 cm (23⅝ x 27⅛ in.)
Printer: Studio PM

800 227 1428   WWW.POMEGRANATE.COM

Pomegranate

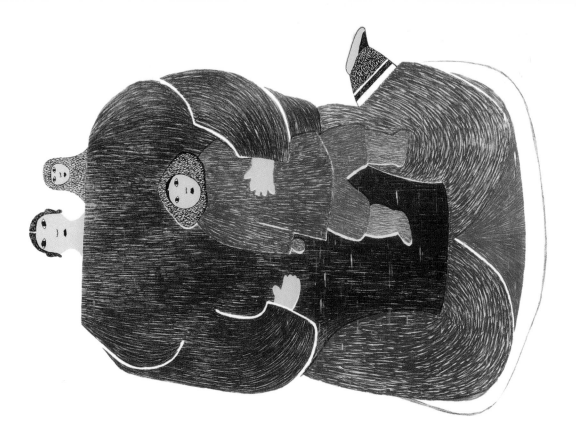

Life on the Land: **INUIT ART FROM CAPE DORSET**

Pitaloosie Saila (Canadian, born 1942)
Mother, 1981
Lithograph, 66.5 x 50.5 cm (26³⁄₁₆ x 19⁷⁄₈ in.)
Printer: Pitseolak Niviaqsi

800 227 1428   WWW.POMEGRANATE.COM

Pomegranate

Life on the Land: **INUIT ART FROM CAPE DORSET**

Kananginak Pootoogook (Canadian, 1935–2010)
Sign of Summer, 2008
Stonecut, 71.5 x 62 cm (28⅛ x 24⁷⁄₁₆ in.)
Printer: Qiatsuq Niviaqsi

800 227 1428   WWW.POMEGRANATE.COM

Pomegranate

Life on the Land: **INUIT ART FROM CAPE DORSET**

Kenojuak Ashevak (Canadian, 1927–2013)
Six-Part Harmony, 2011
Stonecut and stencil, 62 x 99.5 cm (24$\frac{7}{16}$ x 39$\frac{3}{16}$ in.)
Printer: Qavavau Manumie

800 227 1428   WWW.POMEGRANATE.COM

Pomegranate

Life on the Land: **INUIT ART FROM CAPE DORSET**

Kananginak Pootoogook (Canadian, 1935–2010)
Evening Shadow, 2010
Stonecut and stencil, 62 x 99.5 cm (24$^{7}/_{16}$ x 39$^{3}/_{16}$ in.)
Printer: Qavavau Manumie

800 227 1428   WWW.POMEGRANATE.COM

Pomegranate

Life on the Land: INUIT ART FROM CAPE DORSET

Kenojuak Ashevak (Canadian, 1927–2013)
Owl's Consort, 2012
Stonecut and stencil, 62 x 99 cm (24$^{7}/_{16}$ x 39 in.)
Printer: Qavavau Manumie

800 227 1428   WWW.POMEGRANATE.COM

Pomegranate

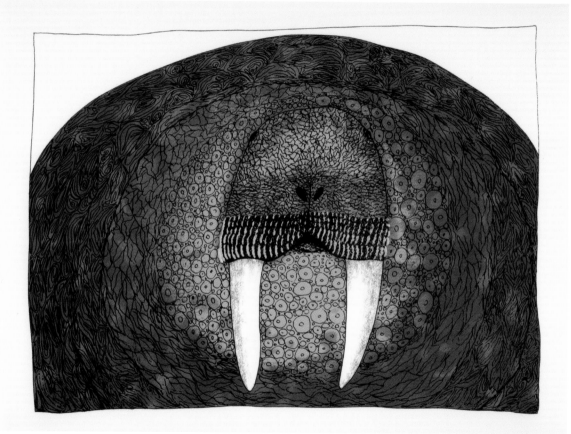

Life on the Land: **INUIT ART FROM CAPE DORSET**

Ningeokuluk Teevee (Canadian, born 1963)
Imposing Walrus, 2009
Serigraph, 38 x 45.7 cm (14^{15}/$_{16}$ x 18 in.)
Printer: Atelier GF

800 227 1428   WWW.POMEGRANATE.COM

Pomegranate